Creative Riddles & Trick Questions For Kids and Family

300 Riddles and Brain Teasers That Kids and Family Will Enjoy!

W9-ATZ-641

Riddleland

Table of Contents

Alert: Bonus Book for the Kids!

FUN RIDDLES
AND
silly jokes
— FOR —
KIDS AND FAMILY

50 bonus
riddles, jokes and funny stories

RIDDLELAND

https://bit.ly/riddlelandbonus

Thank you for buying this book, We would like to share a special bonus as a token of appreciation. It is collection 50 original jokes, riddles and 2 funny stories

RIDDLES AND JOKES CONTESTS!!

Riddleland is having **2 contests** to see who are the smartest or funniest boys and girls in the world!

1) **Creative and Challenging Riddles**
2) **Tickle Your Funny Bone Contest**

Parents, please email us your child's "Original" Riddle or Joke **and he or she could win a $50 gift card to Amazon.**

Here are the rules:
1) It must be challenging for the riddles and funny for the jokes!
2) It must be 100% Original and not something from the internet! It is easy to find out!
3) You can submit both joke and riddle as they are 2 separate contests.

4) No help from the parents unless they are as funny as you.

5) Winners will be announced via email.

6) Email us at Riddleland@bmccpublishing.com

Other Fun Children Books For The Kids!

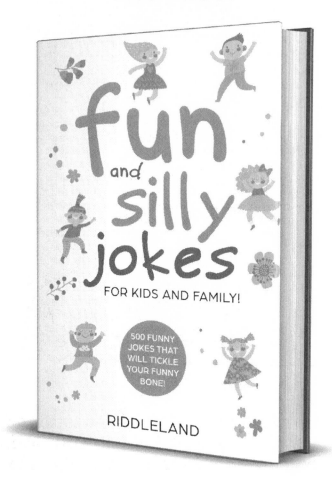

Fun and Silly Jokes for Kids and Family: 500 Funny Jokes That Will Tickle Your Funny Bone!

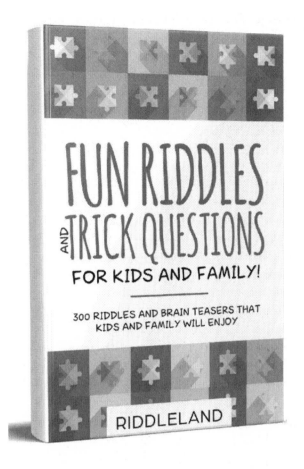

Fun Riddles and Trick Questions for Kids and Family: 300 Riddles and Brain Teasers that Kids and Family Will Enjoy!

Introduction

"We don't stop playing because we grow old; we grow old because we stop playing" – George Bernard Shaw

We would like to personally thank you for purchasing this book. **Creative Riddles and Trick Questions for Kids and Family Book** is the volume 2 of our Riddle Book Series! The book is another collection of 300 fun brain teasers and riddles of easy to hard difficulty.

We received an overwhelming response for the Fun Riddles and Trick Questions for Kids and Family Volume 1 that we want to continue the children's learning and reading journey with volume 2.

These brain teasers will challenge the children and their parents to think and stretch their minds. They have also many other benefits such as:

- **Bonding** – It is an excellent way for parents and their children to spend some quality time and create some fun and memorable memories.

- **Confidence Building -** When parents give the riddles, it creates a safe environment for children to burst out answers even if they are incorrect. This helps the children to develop self confidence in expressing themselves.

- **Improve Vocabulary** – Riddles are usually written in advance words, therefore children will need to understand these words before they can share the riddles.

- **Better reading comprehension** – Many children can read at a young age but may not understand the context of the sentences. Riddles can help develop the children's interest to comprehend the context before they can share it to their friends.

- **Sense of humor** –Funny creative riddles can help children develop their sense of humor while getting their brains working.

Chapter 1: Easy Riddles

"Play is often talked about as if it were a relief from serious learning. But for children, play is serious learning. Play is really the work of childhood." – Fred Rogers

1. Yellow, white and away I go

First you see me in yellow, then you see me in white. Then you see me fly away. What am I?

2. Cow question

How do you spell cow in nine letters?

3. Bumblebee and flower morning

What does the bumblebee say to the wildflower in the morning?

4. Combination bull and a hole

What do you get when you combine a bull and a pit together?

5. Eat to be eaten

When I eat, I can also be eaten. What type of animal am I?

6. White, red, and black

What is white, red, and black all over?

7. A charging rhinoceros

What is the best thing to do if a rhinoceros charges you?

8. Spelling T-Rex

Tyrannosaurus—how do you spell it?

9. One-eyed deer and no tail

What do you call a deer with one eye and no tail?

10. One-eyed deer, no tail, and three feet

What do you call a deer with one eye, no tail, and three feet?

11. Goose immune to snakes

I am a type of goose that a snake's bite cannot affect no matter what happens. What type of goose am I?

12. Running, but not walking?

What can run, but not walk?

13. Making people cry

I am vegetable that makes people cry. The more you cut, dice, chop or slice me, the more tears you will have. What am I?

14. Cars having fun

Where do cars go to ride swings, sit, and go down the slide?

15. What did the juice bottle say to the other juice bottle?

What did the juice bottle say to the other juice bottle that would not shut its mouth?

16. You can't eat this...

What type of apple can you not eat?

17. Forward, but never backwards

What always goes forward, but never go backwards?

18. People use it...

You use me every day but never have to pay for me. I was given to you when you were born. I am very personal to you but I am also shared with everyone. What am I?

19. I never have a shadow...

I never have a shadow before? What am I?

20. People say I am blind.

I am not a person or an animal. I am a feeling. People always say I am blind. What am I?

21. Rabbits favorite place to eat

Where do rabbits go to have their favorite meals for breakfast, lunch, or dinner, and is open 24 hours?

22. I never miss a smell.

I have four noses, so no smells get by me. What am I?

23. Alphabet bones

I have as many bones as the letters in the alphabet. What body part am I?

24. Bean that helps you every morning...

I am one bean that a lot of people need to wake up early in the morning. What type of bean am I?

25. Kangaroo's favorite music

I am the favorite music of the teenage kangaroo. What type of music am I?

26. What number is this?

What number is single no matter how many other numbers it asks to go on a date?

27. Delicious and dangerous

I am a healthy and delicious fruit. Monkey loves me. If you accidentally step on me, you may slip and fall. What am I?

28. Heart located in my head

I live in the ocean. My heart is located in my head, but I'm really small. What animal am I?

29. Roaring like a lion

I can roar like a lion, but my eyes are bigger than the size of my brain. What animal am I?

30. I smell good, but...

If you put a pinch of me on a glass of eggnog, it will smell great. However, if you eat 2 or 3 teaspoons of me raw, you can get sick. What am I?

31. Twin country

If you live in this country, you are most likely to have a twin or know someone who is a twin. What country am I?

32. Diamond rain

I am one of two planets that can produce diamond rain. If Saturn is one of the planets, what planet am I?

33. Light as a feather

I may look light like a feather, but I can weigh up to a million pounds. I change shapes and one of my names is stratus. What am I?

34. Eating a sea vegetable

I am a marine animal that lives in the sea, and I eat with my feet. People call me a sea vegetable. What am I?

35. No life

I can die even though I am not alive. What am I?

36. Yellow and red

I used to be yellow in color, but now I am red in color. Without me, you would crash. What am I?

37. What am I?

You may do this when you are unhappy, but I'm also the name of a group of pugs. What am I?

38. Wrestling president

Before he became president of the United States, this president was the wrestling champion in his county. Who am I?

39. Large dog brain

Compared to the size of their bodies, which dog has the biggest brain out of all the dogs?

40. Pandas and this country

What country owns all the pandas in the world?

41. Venice of the East

Because of its network canal, this city is called the Venice of the East. What city am I?

42. What number am I?

This is the number of hours that children need to sleep every night, as well as the percentage of the world that is left-handed. What number am I?

43. Eat with feet

I am known to have pretty wings, but I eat with my feet. What am I?

44. Impossible to do

If you keep your eyes open, it is impossible to do this. What is it?

45. Can't walk

I have six legs, but I cannot walk. What am I?

46. Giraffe and a refrigerator

How do you put a giraffe into a refrigerator?

47. Less than a penny

I drink nectar, flit around, and weight less than a penny. What am I?

48. Dimples galore

I have over 336 dimples, but I am not living. What am I?

49. Pinch these

People pinch these, they have dimples, and they contain about 10% of human taste buds. What am I?

50. Improving your vision

I am a healthy vegetable. Eating me will help improve your vision. What am I?

51. The more you concentrate...

The more you concentrate, the harder I am to do. What am I?

52. What word?

What word becomes bigger when you add a single letter to the end of it?

53. If an elephant...

What is the name of an elephant's Christmas album?

54. Three syllables

I am the only letter with 3 syllables. What letter am I?

55. A special seat

What type of seat can you flush, and is sometimes made of gold?

56. Fresh pineapple

What state produces over a third of the world's pineapples and only has 13 letters in its alphabet?

57. End of the line

What do you find at the end of every line?

58. Sad math book

What did the sad math book say to its best friend, Mr. Calculator?

59. Yellow sneezes

If sneezes are yellow, what are the color of burps?

60. Kiss flowers

What flowers can kiss really well?

61. Nuts that love money

This type of nut loves money. What nut am I?

62. Policemen's favorite nuts

What are the policemen's' favorite type of nut?

63. Longest flight

The world's longest flight is from this city 'down under' to Dallas, Texas. The flight lasts 16 hours and the city's name could also be a boy's or girl's name. What city am I?

64. Monday through Friday

Why can't Monday through Friday lift weights?

65. Planet Names

I am the only planet that is not named after a Greek god but I am also the only planet with human life. What planet am I?

66. Same size

I am the same size since you were born, but I can also be found on a stove. What am I?

67. Sweet spoiling

I am sweet and I will never spoil. An insect with a sting collects me. What am I?

68. Fast traveling

You cannot see me, but I can travel over 100 miles an hour. What am I?

69. Sleeping skills

A person goes thirty days without sleeping. How is this possible?

70. Old clock

What do you call an old clock?

71. Chewing water

What type of water can you chew?

72. Catch but can't throw

What can you catch, but you cannot throw?

73. To sting or not to sting

What type of bee never stings?

74. Famous actor

Why did the famous actor never sweat?

75. Funny words

What is the most hilarious word in the dictionary?

76. Military recruits

What is the best month for military recruits?

77. Table with no legs

What type of table has no legs?

78. Duck at a restaurant

What did the duck tell the waiter at the restaurant when the waiter bought the duck the check for his five-course dinner?

79. Right eyebrow

What did the right eyebrow tell the left eyebrow?

80. Valentine's Day

When does Valentine's Day fall for single people?

81. Cows drink

If a cow makes chocolate milk and strawberry milk, what kind of milk does a cow drink?

82. What animal is this?

What animal always has money?

83. Hungry clock

How can you tell that the clock is hungry?

84. The magic money book

What book can create money?

85. What is the curviest way?

What is the curviest way to tell time?

86. Sick lemon

What did the doctor give to the sick lemon?

87. Ear that can't hear

What has ears but cannot hear?

88. Furry animal

I am a furry animal and I like to rub against you. But be careful I have long sharp nails. What animal am I?

89. Where does this happen?

Where is the only place that success comes before hard work?

90. Beaver money

Where does the beaver keeps all his money?

91. How many seconds

How many seconds are in February during a leap year?

92. No reptiles

If you are afraid of alligators and pythons, you can to visit me as you'll never find any here! I am the only continent without any reptiles or snakes? Where am I?

93. Born without these

These body parts show up from the ages of 2 to 6 years old, but you are born without them. What body part am I?

94. Only meat

I can't walk, but I only eat meat. I never eat any plants. What am I?

95. The first Macintosh...

The first Macintosh was not a type of computer, but an article of clothing that is popular in Scotland. What type of clothing was it?

96. A country and a tree

I am a country that is named after a tree. I'm in South America, and I have a lot of trees. What country am I?

97. When you put a group of us...

When you put a group of us together, we are called an army, but we do not hurt anyone. What does this group consist of?

98. Alive without a heart

I contain more water than humans. I live in the sea and have no heart. If you touch me, I'll sting you. What am I?

99. One-syllable state

I am on the only state in US with a one-syllable name. What state am I?

100. Shortest sentence

What is the shortest and complete sentence in the English language?

101. Most sung song

I'm only sung once a year, but I am the most sung song in the world. What song am I?

102. Important liquid

I am the most sold liquid in the world, but you do not need me to survive. You can't even drink me. What liquid am I?

103. Dictionary help

What word is always spelled wrong in every dictionary no matter what language?

104. Delicate word

What is the world's most delicate word that when we say it, the word breaks it?

105. US states with Four eyes

Which US state has four eyes and the largest river in US is named after it?

106. What things...

What are the two things can you never eat for breakfast?

107. A mini tree

What tree can you carry in your hand even if your hand is small?

108. Get out of my way

My horn is made out of hair, but if you see me charge, you will get out the way. What animal am I?

109. Fruit shoes

I am a type of shoe that is made from banana peels. What am I?

110. Vegetable shoe strings

This vegetable can help tie your shoestrings. What veggie am I?

111. Ball, but not a ball

I am small like a ball, white and round, but you cannot bounce me. I am use to start fights. What am I?

112. In common

What does Fahrenheit, Lucy, and Celsius all have in common?

113. Big as an elephant

I am as big as an elephant, but I weigh nothing. What am I?

114. Shed or eaten

I am on potatoes, snakes, and humans. I can be shed or eaten. What am I?

115. Cooked with ham

I am a type of vegetable that has a color in my name. I am usually cooked with smoked ham. What vegetable am I?

116. Use us at a large party

People purchase us to use and dispose. We are not edible. We are usually used at large dinner parties. What are we?

117. I fly high

I fly high and fast. I can fly during the day or at night, but when I fly, I do not go anywhere. I usually represent a country. Do you know what I am?

118. Teddy bear

Why does the teddy bear never eat breakfast, lunch or dinner?

119. What are these?

These come out at night and sometimes they do not, but they come out without being called. They also disappear when the sun comes out without being stolen. What are these?

120. December

What does December have that all the other months do not have?

121. Sociable fruit

I am a very sociable fruit, and my social calendar is always booked. What fruit am I?

122. Easy to get into

What can you easily get into, but once you're in it can be difficult to escape?

123. Always in front

What is forever in front of you, but you can never see it?

124. Dependable

When everything goes wrong, you can always count on me. What am I?

125. World traveler

What can travel the world, but at the same time, stay in the same spot?

126. Feel without seeing

You can't see me but you can feel me. In the winter I am cold, while in the summer, I am warm.

127. Talented vegetable

I am the most talented vegetables. Many rappers seek me out. What am I?

128. Provide for you

Everyone has one, animals and humans alike. They provide for you and keep you safe. We celebrate them every May. What are they?

129. Lonely food

What food does not ever want to be alone?

130. I bite

I am freezing cold, and I bite, but I have no teeth. What am I?

131. More popular

I am more popular than real ones, and people get me every year. No matter if I'm real or fake, you can always dress me. What am I?

132. Lots of sides

I am located on two sites of the human body, and I'm also the name of the side of a hammer. What am I?

133. Break easily

You cannot see me or touch me, but you can break me easily. What am I?

134. Like an ostrich

I look like an ostrich, but I cannot walk backwards. What am I?

135. Hyper and late

When you eat me, you can get a burst of energy, but if it is time to make an appointment, I am always late. What am I?

136. Cheese and Fashion

This country is famous for a popular landmark and fashion. It is also the country that consumes the most cheese in the world. Many cheeses are named after different regions in the country. What country is this?

137. What ocean

What did the Pacific Ocean say to the Atlantic Ocean?

138. End of the rainbow

What is at the end of every rainbow?

139. Clumsy

I fall a lot. Some may even say I'm clumsy. However, when I fall, I never get hurt. What am I?

140. Veggie eggs

I may be a vegetable, but if you listen to my name, you will think I grow eggs. What am I?

Chapter 2: Hard Riddles

"For a small child there is no division between playing and learning; between the things he or she does 'just for fun' and things that are 'educational.' The child learns while living and any part of living that is enjoyable is also play." ~ Penelope Leach

141. Drink and I die

If you feed me, I will continue to grow. However, if you give me drink, I will die. What am I?

142. Boy into a man?

What three letters transform a boy into a man? I am the same three letters that can transform a girl into a woman. What are the three letters?

143. Brother's keeper

I will never be your brother, but you will always be mine? Who am I?

144. Numbers

If three is considered a crowd, and two is considered company, what are 5 and 4 considered?

145. Tricky, tricky

There are layers to me. You can hear me in a game or hear me in a construction scene. I am also spelled the same way forward and backwards. What am I?

146. Bad vs good

What smells bad when it is alive, but smells good when it is dead?

147. White and dirty

What gets whiter the more dirty it becomes?

148. Pretend with me

Pretend that you are in the middle of the ocean in a boat. Your boat has a hole in the middle and is slowly sinking. You are surrounded by hungry sharks that haven't eaten in 4 days. What should you do?

149. Two keys

These two keys can never open a door. What are they?

150. Do not ask

Who is always answered, but never asks any questions?

151. Four-letter word

This word has four letters. It can be written upside-down, backwards, or forward and still be read. What word am I?

152. Green stone

If you throw a green stone into a blue sea, what will happen to the stone?

153. Faster

The faster you run, the harder I am to catch. What am I?

154. A son name Jack

I am a king and I have queen. We have a son name Jack. Who are we?

155. A family thing

Mrs. Mary has 4 brothers. Each of her sons has a sister. How many children does Mrs. Mary have in all?

156. All around the house

I run all around the house and sometimes an entire neighborhood, but I never move. What am I?

157. Less than five

I am less than five. The average person in America has this number of credit cards, and a lion can't roar until this age. What number am I?

158. Minus this number

Minus this number is the same number in Fahrenheit and in Celsius. What number am I?

159. World's largest

I am the world's largest ocean, and sometimes people pronounce this word instead of specific. What word am I?

160. The real French fry

You may think French fries were created in France, but they weren't. They were invented in this country, and this country is also known for chocolate. What country am I?

161. Five children

There are five children in a room. Ricky is playing chess. Ivy is relaxing. Perry is eating a cupcake, and Lewis is reading a book. What is Amanda doing?

162. This country

Paper was invented in this country, but tree-hugging is forbidden. The wheelbarrow was also invented in this country. What country is this?

163. What goes here?

What is needed to go through a door, but this item never goes inside or comes out?

164. What can you hold?

What can you hold in your left hand, but not in your right hand?

165. What word?

What word becomes smaller when you add letters to it?

166. 'Mt'

I am the only word that ends in 'mt'. What word am I?

167. Miracle geography

What has forests, but no trees, water, but is not wet, and cities, but no houses?

168. Running fox

What distance can a running fox go into the woods?

169. Same number of letters

I am the only number that has the same number of letters at the number I am. What am number am I?

170. Continent and a country

I am the only country that is also a continent. What country am I?

171. The oddest number

I am known to be an odd number, but if you take one letter away, I become even. What number am I?

172. Leopard

A leopard can change its spots. How is this possible?

173. Unwanted invention

The man who bought this invention does not want it. The man who invented this does not need it. The man who needs this invention does not know he will need it. What invention am I?

174. Only word

What is the only word that starts with 'und' and ends with 'und'?

175. Lisa's mother

Lisa's mother has four children. The first three were named April, May, and June. What is the name of the 4th child?

176. What am I?

You may not hear me often, but I am the English past tense of the word 'dare.' What word am I?

177. Who's first?

A squirrel, a cat, a monkey, and a bird have all climbed up on a mango tree. Who will get to eat the coconut first?

178. Serve me

You can serve me, but you can never eat me. What am I?

179. I go fast

I go fast and a round and a round. I can also be spelled the same way forwards and backwards. What am I?

180. The past

You can find me in the past, but I am being created in the present. However, the future has no effect on me. What am I?

181. Contest winner

There was a contest where you had to hold something. The winner of the contest had no arms or legs. What did the contestants have to hold?

182. I am almost

I am almost perfect because I am the longest word that can be spelled alphabetically in order. What word am I?

183. Jack and the ferret

I went up the hill with this person, and I am also the name of a female ferret. What am I?

184. What am I?

I sleep with my shoes every day. What am I?

185. Long tongue

What has a long tongue, is always ready to walk, but cannot talk?

186. What turns

What can turn everything around without moving an inch?

187. Why not?

A woman living in Tennessee cannot be buried in New York. Why not?

188. Filled with keys

I am filled with keys, but I cannot open a single door. However I can make beautiful sounds. What am I?

189. This name

If you take the first letter of the months, July through November, you get this name. What is this popular boy's name?

190. Starts and ends

What starts with a 'P' and ends with an 'E,' and contains thousands of letters?

191. I am

I am a card name, and the name of the most sensitive finger. I am also found in books. What am I?

192. You need me

You need me to make cornbread and biscuits. I'm a popular milk, but I contain no butter. What milk am I?

193. I'm a sea, but not really

I am a sea, but I'm really a lake. What am I?

194. If...?

If Mary and her cat weren't under an umbrella, why didn't they get wet?

195. What weighs more?

What weighs more? Ten pounds of rocks or ten pounds of feathers?

196. If you do this...

If you do this to someone else, they will laugh and may even snort. However, you can never do this to yourself even if you want to badly. What is it?

197. Guess what I am

I can fly without the use of wings, and I can cry without the use of eyes. Guess what I am.

198. What am I?

I am a ship that was built to ride the biggest waves that life may throw at you. I am not built out of wood but out of actions, minds, and hearts. What am I?

199. I do not eat

I do not eat food, but I enjoy a light meal every day. What am I?

200. Only 1 thumb.

I am made of cloth and I have only one thumb. I am used to carry things that hot. What am I?

201. Everyone needs this

What does everyone need, sometimes asks for it, and often times end up not taking it?

202. Every time I take a bath

I love to take baths, but every time I take a bath, I get smaller. What am I?

203. What's the difference?

What is the difference between a train and the teacher in a classroom?

204. People raise me

People can raise me, change me, earn me, and keep me, even though I can be dirty. What am I?

205. What bone is this?

What bone can get longer and shorter without causing any pain?

206. Four rubber ducks

Four rubber ducks were floating in the bath tub. Two of the rubber ducks drowned and two of the rubber ducks floated away. How many rubber ducks are alive?

207. A young girl and her doctor

A young girl was rushed to the emergency room, but the doctor refused to operate on her. When the doctor saw the child, the doctor said, "This is my niece," but the doctor was not the young girl's uncle. How is this possible?

208. Facing forward

When facing forward, I weigh a whole bunch; when I'm facing backwards, I do not. What am I?

209. What is black?

What is very black when you first buy it, very red when you use it, and ashy gray when you throw it away?

210. I live

I can only be alive where there is light, but if you put the light on me, I automatically die. What am I?

211. I am a mirror

I am a mirror for the rich and famous. I share a lot of information. I can show you the entire world, even though I can be small. What am I?

212. Every evening

Every evening, I am told what to do. In the morning, I do as I was told, but people still get mad at me. What am I?

213. Throw it away

What is it that you can throw away multiple times, but it keeps coming back?

214. Tall or short

No matter if you are tall or short, skinny or fat, you lose me every time you stand up. What am I?

215. What goes down

What can go down a huge hill, but never moves?

216. Which is correct?

Which of the following sentences is correct? 1) An ostrich can fly or 2) Ostriches fly.

217. Buying a rooster

You buy a rooster with the hopes of eating a breakfast of fresh eggs every morning. You expect the rooster to lay 3 eggs every morning and eat 2 eggs every morning. How many eggs will you have remaining after the 10th day?

218. What is this?

What tastes better than the way is smells?

219. A young boy leaves home

A young boy leaves home and turns left three times. When he gets back home, he is facing two men wearing masks. Who are these two men?

220. No parachute

One day, a man decided to jump out an airplane without a parachute. However, when he reaches the ground, he was not injured and was completely safe. How is this possible?

221. Why should you never do this?

Why should you never, ever tell someone a secret in a field full of corn?

222. To prepare me

To prepare me, you must first throw away my outside and then cook my inside. After I am cooked, you will eat my outside and then throw away my inside. What am I?

223. What is the difference

What is the difference between a poorly dressed man on a unicycle and a well-dressed man on a bicycle?

224. Lion in pain and a rainy day

What is the main difference between a rainy day and a lion with a toothache?

225. A lot of clothes and a little clothes

A man in a three-piece business suit fell into a swimming pool. A man in swimming trunks fell into the same swimming pool. They fell at different times, but what is the first thing that happen after both of them fell into the swimming pool?

226. We can tell

We can tell the truth, or we can tell lies. We can poison you without touching you and hurt you without even moving. It does not matter how big or small we are. We can also make lift you up and make your feel better without moving. What are we?

227. A tall hill and a bell

If I stand on a very tall hill and ring a very loud bell between a large house made of wood and a small house made of brick, which house will hear the bell first?

228. What can murmur

What can murmur, but never talk. What runs, but never talks? What has a mouth, but never eats and has a bed but never sleeps?

229. Carrying me

You can carry me whenever you go, but I am not heavy. If you add more of me to the journey, even one million, I will still be the same weight. What am I?

230. A man

A young man was sitting in his luxurious room when he heard a soft knock on the door. When he opened the door, he saw an old man he had never seen before. The old man at the door said, "I'm so sorry. I thought this was my room. I apologize for my mistake." The old man then turned and walked down the hall to the elevator. The young man went back into his room and called security. What made the young man so suspicious of the old man?

231. Accidents

These accidents happen every single day and night. What are they?

232. What can't come in?

What can come all the way to the door of the house, but is never able to enter the house?

233. What is the question?

The answer to this question is yes, but I really mean no. What is the question?

234.This type of kitten

This type of kitten works for the Red Cross. What type of kitten am I?

235. I ask no questions

I ask no questions, but get tons of answers. No matter what time of day, I will always do my job. What am I?

236. I am small

I am quite small. I am only a few inches long and only a couple inches wide. I am worth the weight I am. What am I?

237. A man and his dog

A man and a dog were going down the street. The man rode, yet walked. What is the name of the dog?

238. Different lights

Different lights have an effect on me. My shape changes no matter how dim or bright, no matter if it is day or not. What am I?

239. There was an old man

There was an old man who had a fortune. He had three daughters and wanted to leave the fortune to one of the three daughters, but he didn't know which one to leave the fortune to. So, he came up with a plan. He gave each daughter a few coins and told them to go out and buy something that could fill up their living room. The first daughter bought some sticks, but it was not enough to fill a room. The second daughter bought straw, but it was not enough to fill the room. The third daughter bought two things that were able to fill the room, so she got the father's fortune. What were the two things that the third daughter bought?

240. If a man

If it takes a man one full day to dig a big hole, how many days does it take two men to dig half a whole?

241. What does not leave its roof?

What does not leave its roof, but can row with four oars?

242. What has...?

What has no end, middle, or beginning?

243. Spelled forwards

When spelled forward, I cause a lot of heartache and pain. When spelled backward, I cause lots of joy and happiness. What world am I?

244. Four knees

I can't jump, yet I am the only animal with four knees. What am I?

245. Airplane success

There are no airplanes that had ever arrived safely in Cincinnati. How is this possible?

246. What drink do you get?

What drink do you get when you milk a cow after an earthquake?

247. What number?

When you multiply all the numbers on a cell phone's dialing pad, what number do you get?

248. Basement flooded

When your basement is flooded, what type of shoes should you always wear?

249. A mic

You need a mic and some music to hear me. If done right, I am a thing of beauty, I am word that means 'empty orchestra' in Japanese. What word am I?

250. Beating me

People likes to beat me. Others often like the sound that I makes when I am beaten, and encourage the beating. What am I?

251. What fish is this?

What kind of fish chases mice?

252. A boat

You see a boat filled to capacity with people. The boat isn't sinking, but when you look again, you do not see a single person there. How is this possible?

253. What am I?

What is huge and yellow and pass by the house every morning. When it comes, most moms are very happy. What am I?

254. Birds in a tree

There are 9 birds in a tree. A hunter successfully shot one of the birds down. How many birds are left in the tree?

255. Dropping eggs

A little girl goes to the store and buys a dozen eggs. On the way home, she trips on the sidewalk and all but three break. How many eggs does she have left?

256. Breaks on water only

What only breaks on water, but never breaks on land?

257. Three doctors

Three doctors say that Roberta is their sister. Roberta says that she has no sisters. Who is lying?

258. A woman trapped

A woman is trapped in a room. The room only has two ways to leave: two doors. The first door is home to a fire-breathing dragon. The second door is made out of a magnifying glass which the sun automatically burns to death anyone who enters the door. How does the woman manage to escape?

259. Forgetting your driver's license

An elderly gentleman forgot his driver's license at home. He goes down a one-way street the wrong way. He did not stop for people crossing the road or for any stop signs. A cop is watching him do this but did not give the man a ticket. Why does the policeman not give him a ticket?

260. Plane crash

A plane crashes on the border of the US and Mexico. Where do they bury the survivors?

261. Ten fishes

There are ten fish in a beautiful fish tank. Two of them died. Four swam away and two sank to the bottom. How many fish are left in the beautiful fish tank?

262. Middle of Toronto

What are you sure to find in the middle of Toronto no matter what city you are flying in from?

263. What can you catch?

What can you quickly catch, but you can never throw?

264. Hiding rabbit

There's a rabbit in the forest. It starts raining. Under what type of tree will the rabbit hide?

265. Looking at my face

When you look at my face, you will not see the number 13 at any spot or space. What am I?

266. Cell phone and glasses

Why did the cell phone need a pair of glasses?

267. Dividing among friends

Last week, Wednesday, Julie, and Jennifer went to have breakfast together. They divided the bill equally among themselves when it came time to pay. The total price of the bill was $12. Julie paid $4, and Jennifer paid $4. Who paid the last $4?

268. Traveling and invisible

I travel a lot. I meet rich people and poor people. I go near and I go far. I am invisible, but you can always see what I do. Who am I?

269. What word is this?

There is an English word in which the last three letters is use to form female given titles, the first two letters mean a man, and the first four mean a great man. The entire word by itself means a very great woman. What is this word?

270. Goes up and down

What does up and down, but never moves?

271. What building am I?

I may be a skyscraper, and then I may not. One thing for sure, I contain the most stories in this world. What building am I?

272. What cup does not...

What cup does not hold any water?

273. Who am I?

I have a ring but absolutely no fingers. What am I?

274. Two twins

Two twins, a king and a queen all lay in a large room. How is it that there are no adults in the room?

275. Ten men

I am as strong as ten men, but ten men can never hold me. What am I?

276. Everyone asks

Everyone asks to know the real me. For some, I am a sigh of relief; for others, I am their greatest nightmare. What am I?

277. What work?

What work can one never ever finish?

278. The more

The more of me you have, the less you are able to see. What am I?

Chapter 3: Difficult Riddles

"The activities that are the easiest, cheapest, and most fun to do – such as singing, playing games, reading, storytelling, and just talking and listening – are also the best for child development." ~ Jerome Singer

279. The James

One night, a man receives a call from the police. The police told him that his wife almost died and he should come to the scene of the crime as soon as possiblé. The man is extremely shocked. He drops the phone and drives 45 minutes to the crime scene. As soon as the husband gets there, he is arrested. Why is this?

280. Mad surgeon

A mad surgeon wants to take a person with five heads and take four of the heads off and sew them onto a clown's head. If one head take 90 minutes to be attach to a clown's head, how long would the entire surgery take?

281. A huge house

A huge house is on fire. There are three rooms. The first room is full of rare, antique art. The next room is full of precious diamonds and jewels. The last room is full of money from the bottom of the floor to the top of the ceiling. Which room do the policeman put out first?

282. The magician and a bet

A famous magician is performing his favorite trick of being under water for 10 minutes in front of a large crowd. He completed the trick to and received a standing ovation. However, after the trick, a man in the audience name Luke approaches him and says he can do the same trick as the magician, but he can be under water for 20 minutes. The magician did not believe him and bet Luke $100 that Luke could not stay under water for 20 minutes. Once Luke finished, the magician had to pay Luke $100. How was this possible?

283. Three-digit number

There is a three-digit number. The second digit is as four times as big as the first digit. The last digit is minus three time the second digit. What is this number?

284. Mary and her career choice

Once upon a time, Mary went to her parents and told them that she wanted to shoot and blow people up. She said it happily with a smile on her face. Instead of being shocked, her parents were very proud of her career choice. What did Mary say that she wanted to do?

285. The colorful houses

If a yellow woman lives in a yellow house, a pink woman lives in a pink house, a green woman lives in a green house, a purple woman lives in a purple house, and a blue woman lives in a blue house. What type of woman lives in the white house?

286. In love and apples

A bus driver and a doctor felt in love with the same woman, a beautiful woman by the name of Gina. They often try to woo Gina and gave her all the gifts she wants in the attempt to win her heart. She is polite and gives both of them her affection. The bus driver has to go on a long journey that will last a week, but before he leaves, he gives Gina seven apples. Why did he do this?

287. Verb play

Two young boys were born to the same woman on the same day and on the same year at the same time, yet they are not twins. How is this possible?

288. Your strength

Your strength is the key factor in how far I can go. I have feathers to help me fly, and a head and a body, but I am not alive. You can hold me in your hand, but I am not thrown. What am I?

289. Wet hair

Madison gets into the shower, but when she gets out, her hair is not wet. How is this possible?

290. The odds

Mr. Johnson has two children. One of the children is a girl. What is the percentage of the other child being a girl?

291. Fastest way to drain a tub

You have a gallon water bottle, a teaspoon, and a teacup. What is the fastest way to drain the tub?

292. A dozen stamps

You are in line at the post office because you want to buy 3-cent stamps. When you finally get to the window, you tell the attendant that you want to buy a dozen of 3-cent stamps. How many stamps will you be able to purchase?

293. Cabin in the woods

You are hiking in the woods, and night is quickly approaching. You left all your hiking gear in the car, and it begins to rain. In the distance, you see an abandoned cabin and decide to go inside. Once you get inside, you see a candle, a wood burning stove, and a kerosene lamp. When you look in your pocket, you only see one match. Which do you light first?

294. A barrel of water

There is a big barrel of water that weighs 50 pounds. What must you add to the barrel in order to make it weigh 23 pounds?

295. A family affair

How can all your cousins have an uncle that is not your uncle?

296. Buying a car

A teenager is getting ready to buy his first car. He searched on the internet and found a nice used car for $2500. He visited the owner and was able to buy the car without paying a dime. How is this possible?

297. Painting the house and t-shirts

If you paint a yellow house blue, the house will be blue. If you paint an orange car green, the car will be green. What happens if you throw a white shirt into the Red Sea?

298. Fly in my coffee

A woman orders a cup of coffee at her local diner, but she has a fly in the cup of coffee. She sends the cup of coffee back in order to get a refill. When the coffee returns back to her table, she knew that the waiter gave her the same cup of coffee with a fly in it after taking just one sip. How did she know?

299. The question that is always right

What question can you ask someone at any time, and the answer will always be correct no matter who you ask?

300. A king and his successor

A king has no queen and children. Because of this, he has to choose who will lead his country after he dies. To figure out who will lead after he dies, he gives all the children in his kingdom one seed. The child who is able to grow the most beautiful and largest plant will get to rule the kingdom next. At the end of the contest period, all the children came to the kingdom with the biggest and most beautiful plants one has ever seen. After he looks at all the flowers, he determines that the young girl with the empty pot will be the next ruler of the kingdom. Why did the king choose the little girl over all the people who had beautiful plants?

301. Twenty-five fishes

If you had twenty-five fishes, and five of them drowned, how many fish would you have left?

302. Disappearing number one

How do you make the number one disappear by adding to it?

Chapter 4: Easy Riddle Answers

1.
Answer: A dandelion

2.
Answer: Hamburger

3.
Answer: Hi honey!

4.
Answer: A pit bull

5.
Answer: A fish

6.
Answer: An angry zebra

7.
Answer: You pay the Rhino!

8.
Answer: It. The riddle asked how to spell 'it', not tyrannosaurus.
Ha!

9.
Answer: I have no idea.

10.
Answer: I still have no idea.

11.
Answer: A mongoose

12.
Answer: A drop of water in a leaky faucet. Running water. Get it?

13.
Answer: An onion

14.
Answer: A car park

15.
Answer: Close your cap.

16.
Answer: An iPhone or any Apple products

17.
Answer: Your birthday

18.
Answer: Your name

19.
Answer: A light flame

20.
Answer: Love. Love is blind, get it?

21.
Answer: Hop house

22.
Answer: A slug

23.
Answer: A foot. Your foot has 26 bones.

24.
Answer: A coffee bean

25.
Answer: Hip hop music

26.
Answer: The number one because it is always a single number.

27.
Answer: A banana

28.
Answer: A shrimp

29.
Answer: A male ostrich

30.
Answer: Nutmeg

31.
Answer: Benin. Benin is a small country in West Africa. It has the highest rate of twin births in the world.

32.
Answer: Jupiter. Saturn and Jupiter are both planets that can rain diamonds a centimeter across.

33.
Answer: A cloud

34.
Answer: A sea cucumber

35.
Answer: A battery

36.
Answer: A stop sign

37.
Answer: A grumble

38.
Answer: Abraham Lincoln

39.
Answer: A Chihuahua

40.
Answer: China. They rent them out for a fee of about $1 million USD a year.

41.
Answer: Bangkok

42.
Answer: 10

43.
Answer: A butterfly

44.
Answer: Sneeze

45.
Answer: A dragonfly

46.
Answer: Open the fridge, put the giraffe in, and close the door.

47.
Answer: A hummingbird

48.
Answer: A golf ball

49.
Answer: A cheek

50.
Answer: A carrot

51.
Answer: Sleep

52.
Answer: The word "Large". When you add the letter "r", it becomes "Larger".

53.
Answer: Jungle Bells

54.
Answer: W

55.
Answer: A toilet seat

56.
Answer: Hawaii. The Hawaiian alphabets – Piapa, the Hawaiian alphabet song for kids only consist 13 letters.

57.
Answer: The letter 'e'

58.
Answer: 'I have too many problems.'

59.
Answer: Burple

60.
Answer: Tulips. Tulips sounds like 'two-lips' which can kiss.

61.
Answer: Cash-ews

62.
Answer: Dough-nuts

63.
Answer: Sydney

64.
Answer: They are weak days. (Weak and week sound the same.)

65.
Answer: Earth

66.
Answer: Your eyes and on the stove I am called "stove eyes"

67.
Answer: Honey. Bees collects me from flowers

68.
Answer: A sneeze. Sneezes travel at about 100 miles per hour

69.
Answer: The person only sleeps at night.

70.
Answer: A grandfather's clock

71.
Answer: A water-melon

72.
Answer: The common cold

73.
Answer: A Frisbee

74.
Answer: He had too many fans.

75.
Answer: Hilarious

76.
Answer: March

77.
Answer: A multiplication table

78.
Answer: No, thank you. I already have a bill.

79.
Answer: Why do you look so surprised to see me?

80.
Answer: Valentine's Day fall on February 14th regardless if you are single or not.

81.
Answer: None. Cows do not drink milk. They drink water.

82.
Answer: A buck

83.
Answer: It goes for seconds.

84.
Answer: A checkbook

85.
Answer: You can use an hourglass.

86.
Answer: A medicine called lemon-aid

87.
Answer: An ear of corn

88.
Answer: A cat

89.
Answer: The dictionary

90.
Answer: At the riverbank

91.
Answer: Only one—February 2nd

92.
Answer: Antarctica

93.
Answer: Knee caps

94.
Answer: A snake

95.
Answer: A raincoat

96.
Answer: Brazil

97.
Answer: Frogs

98.
Answer: A jellyfish. Jellyfish is made up of 95% water and don't have a heart.

99.
Answer: Maine

100.
Answer: "Go."

101.
Answer: The Happy Birthday song

102.
Answer: Gas/ Petrol

103.
Answer: Wrong

104.
Answer: Silence. Breaking your silence, get it?

105.
Answer: Mississippi. Mississippi river is the largest river in the United States.

106.
Answer: Dinner and lunch

107.
Answer: A palm

108.
Answer: A rhinoceros

109.
Answer: Slippers

110.
Answer: String beans

111.
Answer: A snowball.

112.
Answer: They all have a temperature.

113.
Answer: The elephant's shadow

114.
Answer: Skin. You can eat potato skins and snakes shed their skins.

115.
Answer: Turnip greens

116.
Answer: Paper plates, cups and plastic silverwares

117.
Answer: A flag

118.
Answer: Because it is already stuffed.

119.
Answer: Stars

120.
Answer: A letter 'D'

121.
Answer: A date

122.
Answer: Trouble

123.
Answer: The future

124.
Answer: Fingers and toes!

125.
Answer: A stamp

126.
Answer: The wind

127.
Answer: Beets

128.
Answer: Mothers

129.
Answer: A pear. (A pear sounds like 'a pair' which means two, which is always more than one. Ha!)

130.
Answer: Frostbite

131.
Answer: A Christmas tree

132.
Answer: A cheek

133.
Answer: A promise

134.
Answer: An emu

135.
Answer: Choco-late

136.
Answer: France. Brie, Camembert, Roquefort are some of the cheeses named after specific regions in France

137.
Answer: Nothing, they just wave at each other.

138.
Answer: The letter 'W'

139.
Answer: Rain or snow

140.
Answer: Egg

Chapter 5: Hard Riddle Answers

141.
Answer: A fire

142.
Answer: Age

143.
Answer: Your sister

144.
Answer: Nine

145.
Answer: Level

146.
Answer: Bacon

147.
Answer: A chalkboard

148.
Answer: Stop pretending!

149.
Answer: A monkey and a donkey

150.
Answer: A loud doorbell

151.
Answer: Noon

152.
Answer: It will get wet and sink to the bottom.

153.
Answer: Your breath

154.
Answer: A deck of cards

155.
Answer: Five. All of the sons have the same 1 sister.

156.
Answer: A fence

157.
Answer: 2

158.
Answer: -40. -40F is the same as -40C

159.
Answer: Pacific

160.
Answer: Belgium

161.
Answer: She is playing chess with Ricky.

162.
Answer: China

163.
Answer: A keyhole

164.
Answer: Your right hand

165.
Answer: Shorter. When you add the letter 'e' and 'r', it becomes smaller

166.
Answer: Dreamt

167.
Answer: A map

168.
Answer: Any distance it wants as long as it does not reach the end.

169.
Answer: 4

170.
Answer: Australia

171.
Answer: Seven. When you take the 's' away, the word becomes 'even.'

172.
Answer: It can move from one spot that it is standing to another spot.

173.
Answer: A coffin

174.
Answer: Underground

175.
Answer: What

176.
Answer: Durst

177.
Answer: None. There are not any coconuts on a mango tree.

178.
Answer: A tennis ball

179.
Answer: A racecar

180.
Answer: History

181.
Answer: Their breath

182.
Answer: Almost

183.
Answer: Jill

184.
Answer: A horse

185.
Answer: A shoe. The strip of leather or cloth material under the shoe laces are called shoe tongue

186.
Answer: A mirror

187.
Answer: The woman is still living.

188.
Answer: A piano

189.
Answer: Jason, J for July, A for August, and so on... Get it?

190.
Answer: The post office

191.
Answer: Index

192.
Answer: Buttermilk

193.
Answer: The Dead Sea

194.
Answer: It was not raining.

195.
Answer: They both weigh ten pounds, so they weigh the same.

196.
Answer: Tickle yourself

197.
Answer: Clouds

198.
Answer: Friendship

199.
Answer: A plant

200.
Answer: A mitten

201.
Answer: Advice

202.
Answer: A bar of soap

203.
Answer: The train says "Chew, Chew," and the teachers says, "Spit your gum in the trash."

204.
Answer: Money

205.
Answer: A trombone

206.
Answer: Zero. Rubber ducks are not alive, so they cannot drown.

207.
Answer: The doctor is the young girl's aunt.

208.
Answer: A ton

209.
Answer: Charcoal

210.
Answer: A shadow

211.
Answer: A television

212.
Answer: An alarm clock

213.
Answer: A boomerang

214.
Answer: Your lap

215.
Answer: A road

216.
Answer: Neither one of these is correct. Ostriches cannot fly at all.

217.
Answer: You won't have any eggs because roosters do not lay eggs.

218.
Answer: Your tongue

219.
Answer: They are the catcher and the umpire. The young boy is playing baseball.

220.
Answer: The man is jumping from an airplane that is parked safely on the ground.

221.
Answer: It is not safe because the corn has ears.

222.
Answer: An ear of corn. To prepare corn, you first have to throw away the outside husk, and cook the kernel. Then you eat the ears on the kernel, and then throw away the cob.

223.
Answer: Attire. Attire sounds like 'a-tire' which is the main difference between a unicycle and a bike. A unicycle has one tire and a bicycle has two tires. Haha!

224.
Answer: One pours with rain and the other roars in pain.

225.
Answer: They both got wet.

226.
Answer: Words. Words can hurt or lift a person up.

227.
Answer: Neither one of the houses. Houses do not have ears that can hear so it is impossible for them to hear the sound.

228.
Answer: A river

229.
Answer: Your name

230.
Answer: You do not have to knock on your own hotel door. You will already have the key. Since the old man did not have a key to the room, the young man became suspicious.

231.
Answer: They are night falls and day breaks.

232.
Answer: The steps

233.
Answer: "Do you mind?" When you say yes to this question, you are really saying 'no.' Hence, a 'yes' answer to this question really means 'no.'

234.
Answer: First-aid kit

235.
Answer: A telephone

236.
Answer: A bar of gold

237.
Answer: The dog's name is Yet.

238.
Answer: The pupil of your eyeball.

239.
Answer: She bought a box of matches and a candle. Once she lit the candle, the light filled the entire room, and that is how she won the fortune.

240.
Answer: None. A half a hole does not exist.

241.
Answer: A turtle.

242.
Answer: A circle

243.
Answer: Desserts. When you spelled desserts backwards, you get stressed.

244.
Answer: An elephant

245.
Answer: There isn't an airport in Cincinnati, Ohio. People in Cincinnati have to cross the states to Kentucky Airport if they want to fly.

246.
Answer: A milkshake

247.
Answer: You get the number 0. When you multiply any number by 0, you get 0.

248.
Answer: Pumps

249.
Answer: Karaoke

250.
Answer: A drum

251.
Answer: A catfish

252.
Answer: The boat is filled with people who are couples, therefore, there are no single people there.

253.
Answer: A school bus

254.
Answer: None. Once the first bird got shot, the rest of the birds flew away because they were scared.

255.
Answer: Three

256.
Answer: Waves

257.
Answer: No one is lying. All of Roberta's siblings are men who are doctors.

258.
Answer: She only leaves at night through the second door when the sun is set.

259.
Answer: The elderly gentleman is walking not driving.

260.
Answer: Nowhere. You do not bury survivors.

261.
Answer: All ten. The fish tank is closed so no fish can leave.

262.
Answer: The letter 'O.' 'O' is in the middle of the word Toronto.

263.
Answer: A cold

264.
Answer: A wet one

265.
Answer: A clock

266.
Answer: It has lost all of its contacts.

267.
Answer: Wednesday was the name of the last friend. And Wednesday paid the last $4.

268.
Answer: The wind

269.
Answer: Heroine

270.
Answer: A staircase

271.
Answer: A library

272.
Answer: A cupcake

273.
Answer: A phone. Phones have ring tones.

274.
Answer: They are all beds, not people.

275.
Answer: Water

276.
Answer: The truth

277.
Answer: Their autobiography

278.
Answer: Darkness

Chapter 6: Difficult Riddle Answers

279.
Answer: The police did not tell him where the crime scene was, yet he showed up. So the husband is the one who tried to hurt his wife.

280.
Answer: This will never happen as nobody humans have 5 heads.

281.
Answer: None. Policeman do not put out fires, firemen do.

282.
Answer: Luke took a glass of water and held it over his head for 20 minutes. As a result, he was able to win the bet.

283.
Answer: The number is 141.

284.
Answer: Mary said that she wanted to be a photographer.

285.
Answer: The President's wife. The First Lady of the United States lives in the white house.

286.
Answer: He did that because of the saying, "An apple a day keeps the doctor away." So the doctor will stay away from his sweetheart.

287.
Answer: They are a part of a set of triplets.

288.
Answer: An arrow

289.
Answer: When she got in the shower, she did not turn the water on.

290.
Answer: 50%

291.
Answer: The usual way. Just unplug the tub, and let it drain the regular way.

292.
Answer: 12 stamps. A dozen is 12.

293.
Answer: You light the match first.

294.
Answer: You need to put holes in it.

295.
Answer: Your dad is their uncle.

296.
Answer: He bought the car for $2500, so he pay the $2500 dollars in dollar bills instead of dimes. A dime is a ten cent coin.

297.
Answer: The shirt will only get wet. The Red Sea is not red, so once you throw the shirt into the Red Sea, the shirt will stay white, but the shirt will be wet.

298.
Answer: Before she sent the coffee back, she had put sugar in it. So when she got the cup of coffee back that was supposed to be new, she could still taste the sugar in her cup of coffee.

299.
Answer: "What time is it?" is the question that is correct no matter who or when you ask.

300.
Answer: The king had given all the children fake seeds that would not grow. The little girl is the only child who was honest and did not switch her seeds out.

301.
Answer: You would have 25 fishes left. Fishes do not drown as they live in water.

302.
Answer: You add the letter 'G' in front of it, so the number one becomes 'gone.' And gone means to disappear. That is how you would do it!

One Final Thing...

Thank for making it through to the end of *Creative Riddles and Trick Questions for Kids and Family*, let's hope it was fun, challenging and able to provide you and your family with all of the entertainment you needed for this rainy day (or sunny afternoon)!

Did You Enjoy the Book?

If you did, please let us know by leaving a review on AMAZON. Review let Amazon know that we are creating quality material for children. Even a few words and ratings would go a long way. We would like to thank you in advance for your time.

If you have any comments, or suggestions for improvement for other books, we would love to hear from and you and can contact us at **riddleland@bmccpublishing.com**

Your comments are greatly valued and the book have already been revised and improved as a result of helpful suggestions from readers.

Alert: Bonus Book for the Kids!

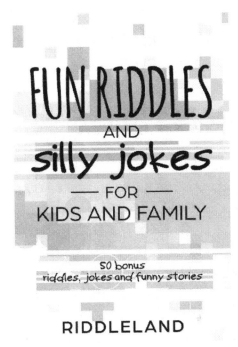

Click here for the Jokes and Stories

Thank you for buying this book, We would like to share a special bonus as a token of appreciation. It is collection 50 original jokes, riddles and 2 funny stories

RIDDLES AND JOKES CONTESTS!!

Riddleland is having **2 contests** to see who are the smartest or funniest boys and girls in the world!

3) Creative and Challenging Riddles

4) Tickle Your Funny Bone Contest

Parents, please email us your child's "Original" Riddle or Joke **and he or she could win a $50 gift card to Amazon.**

Here are the rules:

7) It must be challenging for the riddles and funny for the jokes!

8) It must be 100% Original and not something from the internet! It is easy to find out!

9) You can submit both joke and riddle as they are 2 separate contests.

10) No help from the parents unless they are as funny as you.

11) Winners will be announced via email.

12) Email us at <u>Riddleland@bmccpublishing.com</u>

Other Fun Children Books For The Kids!

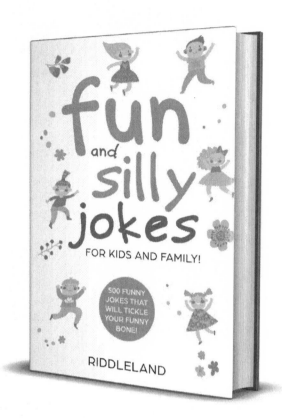

Fun and Silly Jokes for Kids and Family: 500 Funny Jokes That Will Tickle Your Funny Bone!

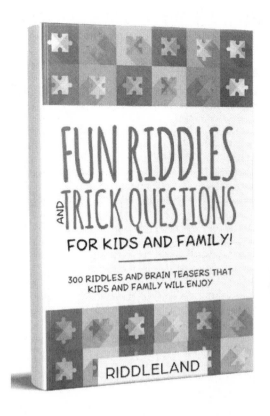

Fun Riddles and Trick Questions for Kids and Family: 300 Riddles and Brain Teasers that Kids and Family Will Enjoy

About the Author

Riddleland is a mom + dad run publishing company. We are passionate about creating fun and innovative books to help children develop their reading skill and fall in love with reading. If you have suggestions for us or want to work with us, shoot us an email at riddleland@bmccpublishing.com

Our family's favorite quote

"Creativity is area in which younger people have a tremendous advantage since they have an endearing habit of always questioning past wisdom and authority."
– Bill Hewlett

Made in the USA
Lexington, KY
13 June 2019